How We Used to Live

Memories of LIFE AT HOME

This photo from 1940 shows children in Birmingham collecting coal for their families from a coal seller. The coal was burned on fires and in ranges.

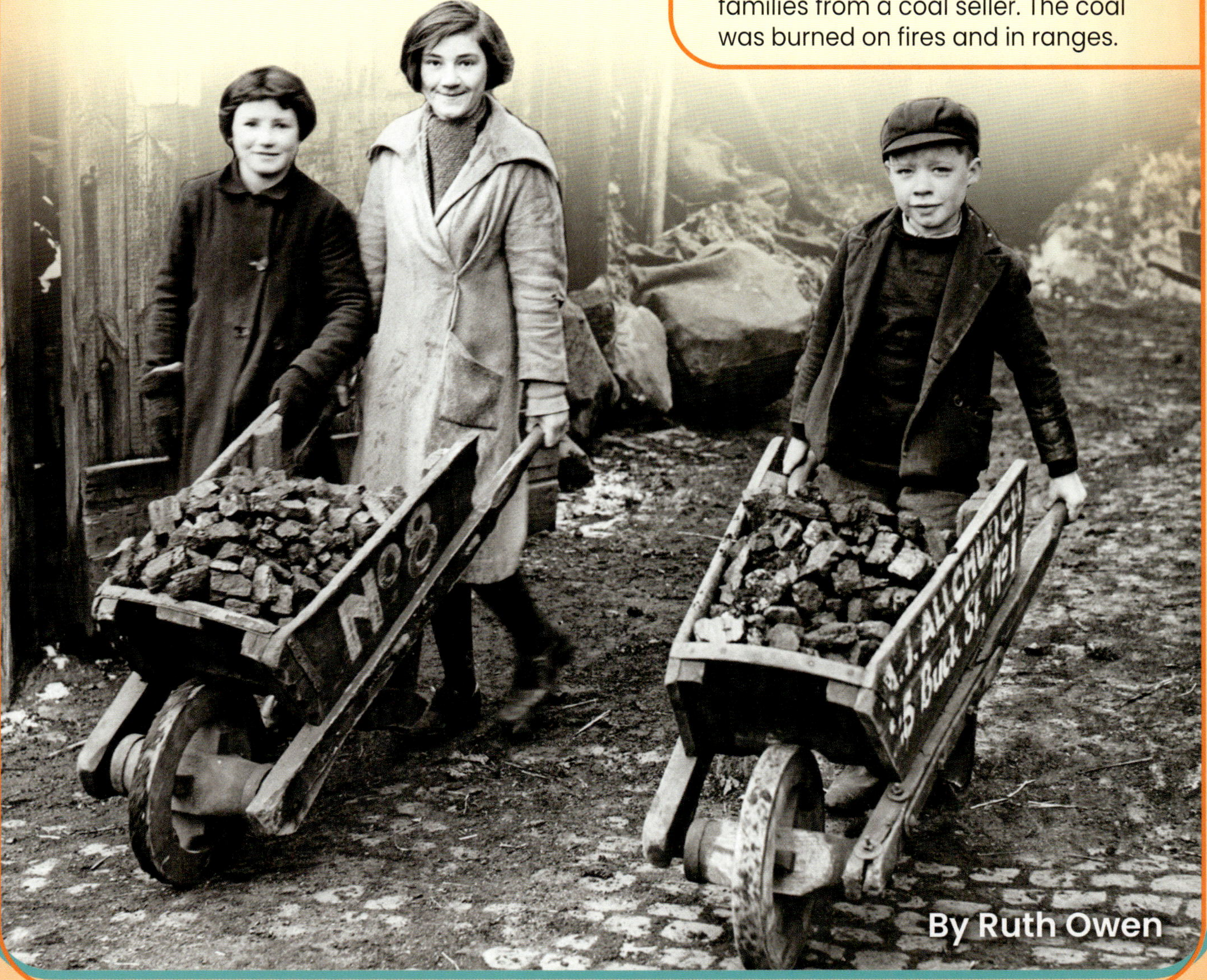

By Ruth Owen

Published in 2025 by **Ruby Tuesday Books Ltd.**

Copyright © 2025 **Ruby Tuesday Books Ltd.**

All rights reserved. No part of this publication may be reproduced in whole or in part, stored in any retrieval system, or transmitted in any form or by any means, electronic, mechanical, photocopying, recording, or otherwise, without written permission from the publisher.

Editor: Mark J. Sachner
Design & Production: Emma Randall

Photo credits:
Alamy: Cover (Trinity Mirror/Mirrorpix), 6 (Pictorial Press Ltd), 7 (Chronicle), 9 (Alan King), 10 (Shawshots), 11TR (Pump Park Vintage Photography), 13T (Trinity Mirror/Mirrorpix), 19T (Sueddeutsche Zeitung Photo), 21 (Heritage Image Partnership); Public Domain: 22; Ruby Tuesday Books: 11B, 14T, 16B, 17T; Shutterstock: Cover (Panda 3800/TravelPOIs.de/Nagel Photography/Kovaleva_Ka/David Fowler), 4L (arslaan), 4R (John Gomez), 5TL (bonchan), 5TR (Taljat David), 5BL (Sarah2), 5BC (Lucie Lang), 5BR (Jason Deines), 8 (Silvia73), 11TL (Photoongraphy), 11B (David Fowler), 12 (slowmotiongli), 13B (Panda 3800), 14C (titelio), 14B (Simon Mayer), 15T (Ivan Protsiuk/Kovaleva_Ka), 15B (New Africa/Kev Gregory), 16B (MaraZe/MR.Phakpoom Mahawat), 17B (Yaroslaff), 18 (Andy J Billington), 19B (TravelPOIs de), 20 (Martin Charles Hatch); Superstock: 23 (ClassicStock).

British Library Cataloguing in Publication Data (CIP) is available for this title.

ISBN: 978-1-78856-421-2

Printed in Poland by L&C Printing

www.rubytuesdaybooks.com

CONTENTS

Looking into the Past 4

Living in a Tenement 6

Using the Privy 8

Living with Rationing 10

Chickens in the Backyard 12

Special Food Treats 14

A Teatime Takeaway 16

Wash Day for Women 18

It's Bath Night 20

The Queen's on TV! 22

Glossary, Index, Answers 24

LOOKING INTO THE PAST

In this book, we are going to look at some **historical** photographs. They capture moments in Britain during the first half of the 1900s.

We will also hear the real-life **memories** of people who lived through some of the times in the photos.

And we will look at objects from the **past** that people once owned and used.

Together, photos, memories and objects can help us to learn how we used to live.

Look at the photos on these pages. What do you think each object is?
(The answers are on page 24.)

What Is a Century?

We measure history in periods called **centuries**. A century lasts for 100 years. Today, we are in the 21st Century.

1801 to 1900	**1901 to 2000**	**2001 to 2100**
19th Century	20th Century	21st Century

3

4

Many of the photos in this book are from a time that we call "living history". It's a time that people who are still alive today can remember.

5

6

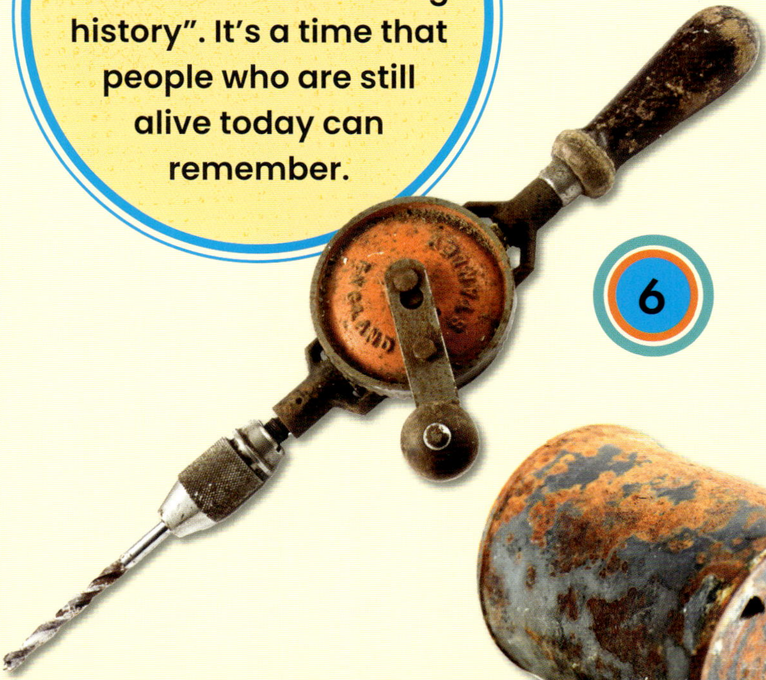

7

LIVING IN A TENEMENT

This photo shows a family living in a tenement flat in 1915.

In the early 1900s, many people lived in terrible poverty in **rented** homes called tenements. Some tenements were also known as **slums**.

The tenement buildings were divided into 10 or more one-room flats.

The roofs often leaked, the walls were crumbling and the windows might have no glass.

A whole family lived in each flat cooking, washing and sleeping in one room.

Children in a London slum in 1910

Women had to work hard to keep their flats clean and homely.

Babies and young children shared their parents' bed.

Each tenement building had one outside tap or pump where people could collect cold water. It also had just one outdoor toilet that might be shared by up to 40 people!

A coal-fired range for heating, cooking and boiling water

USING THE PRIVY

From the 1800s until the 1960s, many homes had outside toilets that were known as privies.

Whether it was raining, snowing or dark, if you needed to go, you had to go outside!

Some toilets were simply a wooden box with a hole to sit on. A bucket beneath the hole caught the pee and poo.

To avoid going outside in the middle of the night, some people used a chamberpot, which they kept under their bed.

John (Born 1940)

" Every morning it was my job to empty my family's chamber pots into the slop bucket. Then I took the bucket outside and poured the slop down the privy. "

A chamber pot was also known as a jerry, a guzunder or a po.

LIVING WITH RATIONING

At the start of **World War II**, lots of Britain's food came from other countries by ship. The Germans tried to sink these ships.

To avoid food shortages, the British government introduced rationing. This made sure that every person had a fair share, or ration, of many types of foods.

This is an adult's ration for one week.

Fruits and vegetables weren't rationed and people grew as much as they could.

The government gave each adult and child a ration book of coupons.

At a food shop, the coupon showed how much of each food a person could buy.

People used carrots instead of rationed sugar to make marmalade, fudge, cakes and Christmas pudding. And when there wasn't enough sugar to make ice cream, children ate iced carrots on sticks instead!

Rationing ended in 1954.

Week 1
One ration of bacon and ham

Coupons

CHICKENS IN THE BACKYARD

In London's East End area there was once a live animal market.

Customers could buy songbirds, pigeons, parrots, kittens, puppies, rabbits, squirrels, goats and monkeys. It was even possible to find a lion cub for sale!

Many of the animals at the market were treated badly and it was closed down in 1983.

In the photo, people are choosing chicks to take home to raise as meat or for laying eggs.

In the 1940s, chicken was an expensive, **luxury** food.

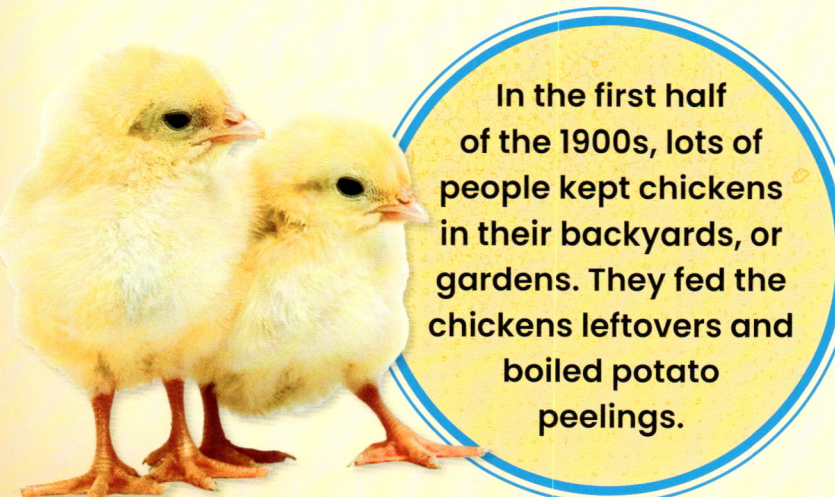

In the first half of the 1900s, lots of people kept chickens in their backyards, or gardens. They fed the chickens leftovers and boiled potato peelings.

Club Row Market, London (1945)

Boxes of chicks for sale

Evelyn (Born 1943)

"Every spring, Dad brought home two chicks. I liked to play with them on the kitchen table. Once they were cockerels, they would chase and peck me. Then, in December, the cockerels disappeared. As a child, I never realised that the roast chicken we ate at Christmas was our cockerels!"

SPECIAL FOOD TREATS

People who grew up in Britain during the 1940s and early 1950s experienced rationing. Some also lived in poverty. However, many have good memories of their favourite food treats.

John (Born 1940)

"My favourite meal was bread and dripping sprinkled with lots of salt and pepper. Some people called it a "mucky fat sandwich"."

When a joint of beef or pork is roasted, fat and juices gather in the pan. As they cool down, they become jelly-like and are known as dripping.

Brenda (Born 1941)

"During the war, no bananas came to Britain on ships. Then one day in 1946, Mum heard that a stall in the market had some. We queued for an hour and each family could buy just one banana. I was five years old and I'd never seen or tasted this fruit before!"

Evelyn (Born 1943)

"As a special treat, Mum would give us a teaspoon of sugar, one of cocoa powder and one of baby milk powder. We ate little amounts with teaspoons or dipped our fingers into the powder and licked it off."

Before the 1960s, few families had freezers. To make food last longer, people **preserved** vegetables in jars of vinegar. Fruits were made into jams or stored in jars and bottles of sugary water. The preserved foods were kept in a large, walk-in cupboard called a pantry or larder.

Preserved foods last for about a year.

Preserved peaches

Cooked ham

Steve (Born 1955)

"One Saturday, there was a large ham in Nan's larder. Grandad shot rabbits in the fields and then sold them at the market. He bought the ham with the money he made. Nan cut me a slice of ham and I ate it with one of her bottled peaches. I'd never eaten anything so delicious."

A TEATIME TAKEAWAY

In the 1940s and 1950s, winkles were a popular Sunday night tea.

Workers collected winkles from the seashore and from the banks of rivers like the Thames.

Once the winkles were boiled in salty water, they were ready to be sold.

A winkle seller measured the little shellfish using a pint beer mug and put them in a paper bag.

To eat this teatime treat, people used a pin to pull the slug-like winkles from the shells.

People ate winkles with brown bread and butter and lots of vinegar and pepper.

Winkles in their shells

Cooked winkles

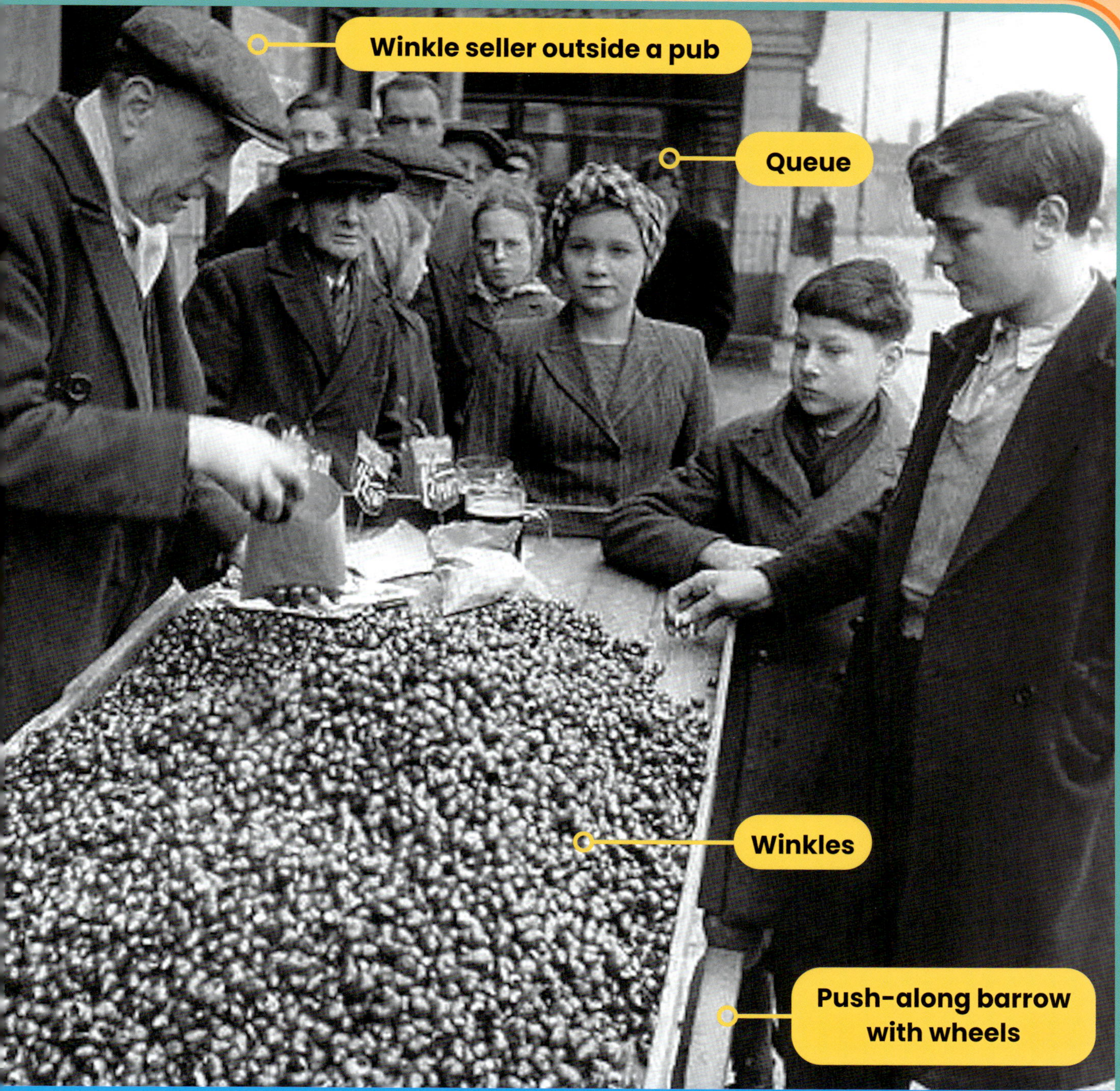
Winkle seller outside a pub
Queue
Winkles
Push-along barrow with wheels

Betty (Born 1942)

"Once I was six years old, it was my job to collect the winkles on Sunday afternoon. It was thruppence, or three old pennies, for a pint. Mum would give me a threepenny bit to pay for them."

THREE PENCE
1943

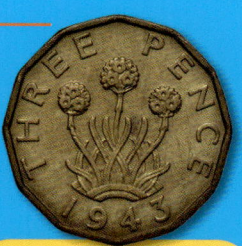

Threepenny bit coin

WASH DAY FOR WOMEN

In the first half of the 1900s, Monday was wash day for many women.

Dirty sheets, towels, tablecloths, clothes, underwear and even snotty handkerchiefs were all washed by hand.

Water was heated in a large, metal cauldron that was called a **copper**. Some items were boiled in the copper.

Other items were put in tubs of soapy water. They were rubbed up and down against a washboard to remove stains.

More tubs were filled with clean water for rinsing.

Then the washing was fed through the rollers of a mangle to squeeze out all the water.

A mangle

Rollers for squeezing

This wheel turned the rollers.

IT'S BATH NIGHT

Before the 1960s, many homes in Britain did not have a bathroom.

People washed each day in a sink or using a bowl of water.

But once a week, usually on Saturday or Sunday, it was bath night!

A large tin bath was dragged in from the backyard and placed in front of the fire.

Then the bath was filled with kettles and saucepans of water that were heated in the copper or on the range.

A bar of soap was used for washing your skin and hair.

Bath night in the 1950s

The youngest member of the family bathed first. Older brothers and sisters went next, then mum and finally dad – all using the same water!

Range

Tin bath

Bucket for emptying the bath

Steve (Born 1955)

"We emptied the bath by scooping the cold, dirty water into a bucket using a saucepan. Then the water was poured onto Dad's potato or tomato plants in the garden!"

THE QUEEN'S ON TV!

In 1953, Britain was excited for the coronation of Queen Elizabeth II. The event would be shown live on television.

Hundreds of thousands of people decided to buy or rent their first TV to see their new queen crowned.

People who didn't have their own TV set gathered around a friend or neighbour's.

More than 20 million British people watched the coronation live on TV.

For many it was the first time they had ever watched television!

Queen Elizabeth II's coronation on TV, 2nd June 1953

All TV in Britain was black and white until 1967.

In the early 1950s, Britain had just one TV channel – the BBC.

Tiny screen

Television set

In the early 1950s, the TV screen went blank each night between 6:00 and 7:00 pm. This was to help parents get their young children to stop watching and go to bed.

Evelyn (Born 1943)

"We were the only family in our street that had a TV. On coronation day our neighbours took turns to squeeze into our little back room to watch the queen. I can't imagine how many sandwiches and pots of tea my mum must have made that day!"

GLOSSARY

century
A period of 100 years.

copper
A large, metal, cauldron-like bucket used for heating water. A coal fire was lit below the copper.

historical
From history, or the past.

luxury
Something that is an extra or a treat and is often expensive.

memory
Something remembered from the past.

past
A time that has already happened.

preserve
To treat something, such as food, in a special way to stop it rotting, or going bad.

rented
Something that is owned by someone else and you pay that person to use it.

slum
A dirty, overcrowded place that is home to people who live in poverty.

World War II
A major war that lasted from 1939 to 1945. It was fought between the Allies (Britain, France, the United States, the Soviet Union and others) and the Axis powers (Germany, Italy and Japan).

INDEX

A
animals 12–13, 15, 16–17

F
food 10–11, 12–13, 14–15, 16–17, 23

H
homes 6–7, 8–9, 12–13, 15, 18–19, 20–21, 22–23

Q
Queen Elizabeth II 22–23

R
rationing 10–11, 14

T
television 22–23
tenements 6–7
toilets 7, 8–9

W
washing and baths 6, 18–19, 20–21
World War II 10

Answers pages 4–5: 1: A telephone from around 1910. **2:** A Box Brownie camera from 1958. **3:** A piece of tripe, which is the lining of a cow's stomach. People ate tripe cooked or raw with vinegar. **4:** A bedwarmer. The round section was filled with hot coals from the fire. **5:** A toasting fork for holding a slice of bread close to an open fire to make toast. **6:** A drill from the 1950s that was powered by turning the handle. **7:** A 1950s tin can pierced with holes so it could be used as a watering can in a garden.